Wings of Fire

Mattie Shavers Johnson

Is there ever victory in or after war?

International Standard Book Number: 0-9620115-4-1

Library of Congress Card Catalog Number: 93-84609

Printed in the United States of America

Post Oak Publications
P. O. Box 70455
Nashville, TN 37207-0455
(615) 227-4562

Permission

Illustrations by James Threalkill except where noted.

The Exodus. © Copyright 1964, Royal Publishers, Thomas Nelson, Inc., Nashville, Tennessee. Reproduced by Permission. Page xiv; 22.

Mosque at Mt. Moriah. © Copyright 1976, 1975, 1971, 1965, 1964 Thomas Nelson, Inc., Nashville, Tennessee. Reproduced by Permission. Page 2.

Cedars of Lebanon. © Copyright 1976, 1975, 1971, 1965, 1964 Thomas Nelson, Inc., Nashville, Tennessee. Reproduced by Permission. Page 2; 136.

Mosque of the Ascension on the Mt. of Olives. © Copyright 1976, 1975, 1971, 1965, 1964 Thomas Nelson, Inc., Nashville, Tennessee. Reproduced by Permission. Page 3.

A Piece of Material (Designer Unknown). "Wings of Fire" (title assigned by author). Page 6; 64; 108.

Children of Palestine by Charles W. Johnson, Jr. (1989). Reproduced by Permission. Page 14.

The Papyrus, "Reed Song." © Copyright 1964, Royal Publishers, Thomas Nelson, Inc., Nashville, Tennessee. Page 14.

Potential Air Strike Targets. Associated Press. © Copyright Wide World Photos, Inc., 50 Rockefeller Plaza, New York, NY 10020. Reproduced by Permission. Page 30.

Church of Gethsemane, Site of the Garden. © Copyright 1976, 1975, 1971, 1965, 1964 Thomas Nelson, Inc., Nashville, Tennessee. Reproduced by Permission. Page 34.

Church in Bethlehem over Site where Christ Was Born by Charles W. Johnson, Jr. Reproduced by Permission. Page 34.

Ships in Persian Gulf and Oil on Water by author from personal collection. Page 38.

Oil on Water by author from personal collection. Page 38.

Men at Conference Table by Charles W. Johnson, Jr. Reproduced by Permission. Page 44.

Tanks Coming Over Hill. Associated Press. © Copyright Wide World Photos, Inc., 50 Rockefeller Plaza, New York, NY 10020. Reproduced by Permission. Page 48.

Tomb of The Virgin Mary. © Copyright 1964, Royal Publishers, Thomas Nelson, Inc., Nashville, Tennessee. Reproduced by Prmission. Page 54.

Eclipse of a Particle: The Vera S. Chatman Collection. Reproduced by Permission. Page 60.

Women at The Wall by Charles W. Johnson, Jr. Reproduced by Permission. Page 62.

Dome of the Rock by Charles W. Johnson. Reproduced by Permission. Page 68.

Bedoin Camp by Charles W. Johnson, Jr. Reproduced by Permission. Page 72.

Livestock on the Sea of Galilee. © Copyright 1976, 1975, 1971, 1965, 1964 Thomas Nelson, Inc., Nashville, Tennessee. Reproduced by Permission. Page 74.

Men Surrender. Associated Press. © Copyright Wide World Photos, Inc., 50 Rockefeller Plaza, New York, NY 10020. Reproduced by Permission. Page 84.

Babylonian Brick. © Copyright 1964 by Thomas Nelson,Inc., Nashville, Tennessee. Reproduced by Permission. Page 88.

Destruction (Oil on Canvas) by author from personal collection. Page 104.

Fire Dance (Oil on Canvas) by author from personal collection. Page 132.

Freedom (Oil on Canvas) by author from personal collection. Page 140.

Is There Ever Victory After War?

Is there ever victory in or after war? Only time will tell:

When the human heart has healed;

When love has been revealed;

When greed has vanished beyond earthly things;

And birds are free to sing.

– *MSJ*

To God's

healing grace;

to my parents:

Robert Stanley Shavers

and Laura Garland Shavers;

and

to faith,

love and forgiveness

This book is also dedicated to my loving husband, Charles W; to my children: Charles W. Jr., Phillip and Livette. It is also dedicated to my twin sister Millie who kept urging me to continue my writing and to complete this book and to my other siblings, Iverson, Myrtle, Mildred and Jenna. It is especially dedicated to members of the United States military personnel who have participated in wars fought on this continent and abroad: Col. John Garland, Capt. James P. Shavers, Lieut. Col. Iverson E . Shavers, Col. Charles Young, Sm 1/C. Charles W. Johnson, Lieut. Charles W. Johnson, Jr., M Sgt. Stanley Shavers, E-5 Theodore Shavers, Pfc. Robert L. Shavers, M Sgt. Lorenzo Shavers, Leonzo Shavers (Marine), Sp-5 Hazel Shavers, Corp. Pauline Shavers, E-4 Carmen Shavers, Sfc. Barmus Benton, Lieut. Garfield Kington, Sgt. Bernard Downs, Sgt. James Shavers, Sgt. Ulysses Shavers, Sgt. Herman Robinson, Norman Hubbard (Seaman), Sgt. General Woodard, Walter Jackson (Air Force), Robert Jackson (Air Force), Sgt. Albert V. Marshall, Alvin Collins (Air Force), Sgt. Val Homer Collins, Lieut. Dawn Gloria Shavers, Sgt. Major Shavers, Capt. Robert Benton, Capt. Michael Shavers, E-5 Blain Shavers, Sgt. Danny House, John House (Army), Sgt. Chauncy Garland, M/SOT Roscoe Shavers, Sgt. Lewis William Shavers, Sgt. James Dillard, Sgt. Jay Hubbard, Corp. Carlos Shavers, Preston Shavers (Army), Corp. George Johnson, Sgt. Ergle Johnson, Sgt. Paul L. Johnson, Corp. Lorenzo P. Johnson, Corp. O. W. McPeters, Sgt. C. Hubbard, Sfc. H. K. Walker, Corp. Q. T. Swink, Sgt. Charlie Shavers, II, Corp. Adrain King, Sgt. Clenton Scott, Devitt Scott (Army), Sgt. Lewis Germany, Sfc. Iverson Bell, Pvt. James H. Garland, Jimmy H. Vaughn (military personnel), and to the million other military personnel of this land.

Contents

Acknowledgments

The author wishes to acknowledge with deep appreciation:

The Tennessean newspaper staff, Frank Sutherland, Editor and C. W. Johnson, Jr., Managing Editor, for advice on securing some photographs.

Many of the inspirational poems in this volume are credited to reading Scriptures from the King James Version of the Holy Bible. Also special appreciation: to my wise, articulate and patient consultant and editor, Emma J. Wisdom, to my friend and mentor, Dr. Vera S. Chatman who allowed me to work and think when I needed it most; to Dr. Chatman's staff, Marti Rosenberg, Elaine Prather and Rotressa Yelling; to Ms. Audrey Hall who provided my first lead to an editor; to Mrs. Sharon Hurt who has been very helpful; and to my pastor, Reverend William A. Alexander who never ceased to remind me that God loves all His children. Without the invaluable assistance of all, this volume of poetry could not have been completed.

Preface

Wars are fought on many fronts. This book of poems was written after the untimely death of the author's brother and mother-in-law. In less than a year earlier, another brother and sister had died. For this reason, this book is sometimes referred to by the author as a "fall-out occurrence" in and after battle.

Work is a great healer, for some. It aids in the process of overcoming great sorrow and despair; and it sometimes results in creativity. The author hopes this work will provoke thought, but most of all, that it will demonstrate that pain is universal – remembering that the prospect for peace is always present if one reaches out to others and invokes God's forgiveness.

Exodus

Mediterranean Sea
Delta
Zoan
(Tanis)
GOSHEN
Succoth
Wilderness of Shur
Wilderness of Paran
Wilderness of Etham
Kadesh-
barnea
CANAAN
Jerusalem
Heshbon
Jahaz
Dibon
AMMON
MOAB
Ije-
abarim
Punon
EDOM
Wilderness
of Zin
SINAI
PENINSULA
Marah
Wilderness
of Sin
Hazeroth
Taberah
Mt. Sinai
Ezion-geber
Elath
EGYPT
(MIZRAIM)
Gulf of Suez
Gulf of Aqaba
MIDIAN
D E S E R T
THE EXODUS
Red Sea
1
2
3
4
5

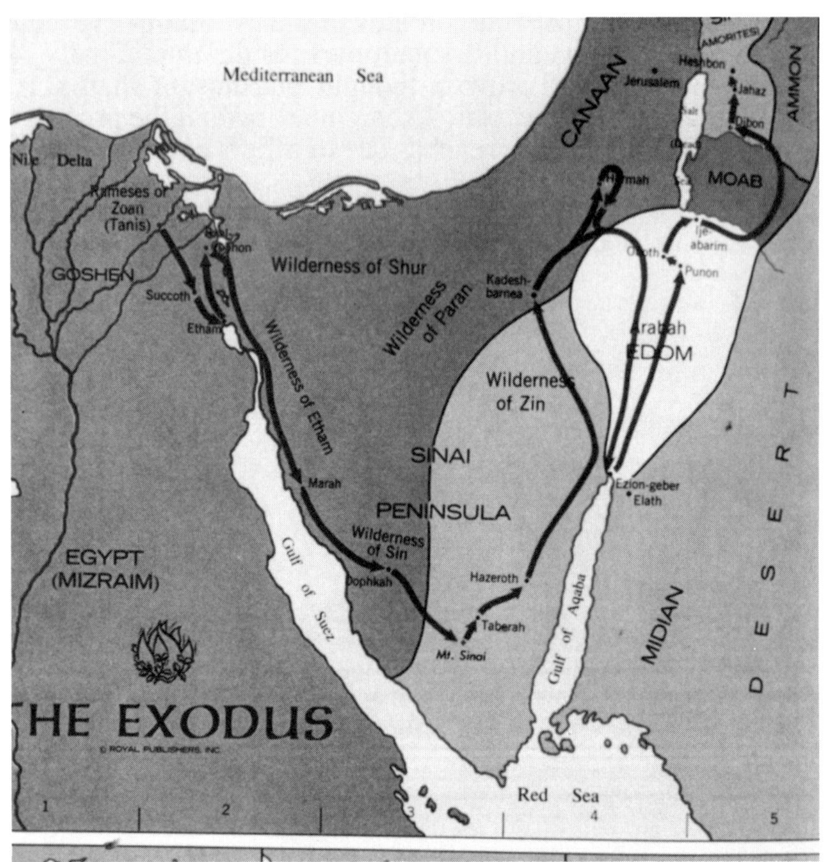

Trade Routes

Tower of Babel

Introduction

The King James Version of the Holy Bible tells us that Babylon (Confusion), the Metropolis of the Babylonian Empire was built on both sides of the Euphrates (in the Valley of the Tigers and the Euphrates). It is also called Babel because of the "stepped tower." The descendants of Noah built a tall stepped tower intended to reach to heaven. God punished the builders by causing each builder to speak in a different language (they were too presumptuous). They became confused and scattered and could not understand each other.

Babel was created about 2230 B.C. It was said to have been one of the largest and most magnificent cities that existed: Fifty-six miles in circumference, covering about two-hundred square miles. It was founded by Nimrod taken by Cyrus and again by Alexander the Great. It gradually fell into ruins. Babylon is mentioned two-hundred and fifty times in the Bible. Some of the locations are: II Ki, 17:30; 20:17; 25:25; I Cor. 9:1; II Chr. 32:31; 56:7; E2 5:12; 7:9; Ps. 87:4; 137; Isa. 14:4, 22:21;9, among others.

Babylon is often referred to as the doomed city, but it was during Nebuchanezzars' reign that it attained its highest splendor. In B.C. 606 Nebuchanezzar carried to Babylon many of the people of Judah including David the prophet. This was the beginning of seventy years captivity set forth by the prophet. In B.C. 587 Nebuchanezzar overthrew Jerusalem. The people were taken to Babylon. Babylon was overturned by Persians B.C. 538. In B.C. 536 by decree of Cyrus, exiles were permitted to return to Jerusalem and rebuild their temple. After the second expedition, those who did not return to Jerusalem were spoken of as the "Dispersed" (Jno, 7:30).

"Kuwait is an independent Arab sheikdom in Eastern Arabia on the Persian Gulf, which was under British protection until 1961. It is six thousand square miles; population, two-hundred six thousand. The capital population is one-hundred five thousand" (Webster's Dictionary, College Edition 1962, The World Publishing Company).

Iraq and Kuwait are located in the general area described above. The area is woven in the history of the Israelites. The history of this area is of war, destruction, advance and retreat.

For centuries, conflict in the Middle East has been rampant and seemingly a way of life.

Biblical Scriptures tell us that Cain slew Abel. But even before, brother was against brother; friend against friend; and nation against nation coupled with greed, jealousy and bloodshed. Bloodshed occurred when King Herod ordered soldiers to go to Bethlehem and kill every male child under two years of age. Many other blood sheddings later led to the eventual crucifixion of Jesus Christ. These events have been steeped in a "power struggle" with overtones of religious roots and beliefs.

Before the technological process of drilling for oil was discovered and perfected, the "ships of sand" moved over the desert seeking more and more goods and services sometimes capturing, enslaving and destroying everything along the way.

This particular conflict—The Persian Gulf War—was spearheaded by a greedy terrorist, namely, Saddam Hussein and other Iraqi officials who enslaved, killed, and attempted to take over Kuwait and its people. Iraq had destroyed Kuwait's property. Seven-hundred-thirty-two oil wells had been blown up, and in an act of vengeance, six million barrels of oil were dumped into the Persian Gulf.

From history, the Iraqis claim Kuwait belonged to them. They attempted to reclaim it. Oil, a precious commodity of Kuwait's, was deemed "power" to the rest of the world. Other neighbors, as this writer interprets, became concerned and involved because their own perceived power and economies were at bay or being threatened. They rationalized involvement as their duty to protect their own interest—a very small nation was being "bullied." Nations rallied to the rescue of Kuwait.

The world has become one community. What affects one, affects us all. We are co-dependent, but we tend to seek out our own agendas. The "fall-out" overwhelms us all.

About the Book

Consequently, the main thrust of this book of poems is about war and its effects. It is a rendition in poetic expression particularly concerning the Persian Gulf War, but also how the war deeply impacts the lives of individuals: The pain, fear and final hope and dreams for a better tomorrow. The book expresses empathy for many parents whose sons and daughters have participated in war – to fight and die in a desert and kill innocent people. It also expresses pain of those not in battle, but left behind to grieve and to wonder about technology that brings war into their living rooms without a place to run or hide.

Further, this book seeks to address the destruction of one of the most beautiful places on the face of the earth; its history and the need for one nation to dominate another. It is about the hopes and dreams of a people; the release from pain at the end of battle and final surrender. It sometimes touches on political and spiritual issues facing us each day and the beauty that strives beyond destruction while coping with the reality of it all.

It should be pointed out at the outset that there has never been any doubt about American support of its military personnel once war was declared and became inevitable. The people of this continent were one-hundred percent; behind our service men and wom en. We were anxious to get it over and looked forward to a better day with as little suffering as possible. And so it was.

This collection of poems has been divided into seven parts, chronicling the Persian Gulf War from roughly the time the American people realized the impending threat of war, landing of military personnel in the Middle East to combat, conclusion and the period shortly thereafter. Hence this collection:

1. Before the Storm.
2. Early Hours of the Storm.
3. Waiting and Hoping for the Best.
4. The Fighting Begins.
5. The fighting Ends.
6. After the Storm.
7. Continued Global Unrest and Destruction.

From ancient times in the Persian Gulf area the flamingo has been referred to as *phenicopter*, "Wings of Fire."

War!

War!

War!

War!

What are we fighting for?

More!

More!

More!

Global destruction to dust –

Fear!

Passion!

Lust!

Part I
Before the Storm

Cedars of Lebanon

Mosque at Mount Moriah. David bought this land for the temple which Solomon built.

Mosque of the Ascension on the Mount of Olives. A consecrated place for Jews, Christians, and Moslems.

Trade Routes

Greed

You pick and choose on
the waterfront.
Like a crane, you
wade in thirst ready for the
hunt,
Harvesting somewhat
indiscriminately
A pouch to be filled
immediately.
Deeper and deeper
determined willed
Till gold rays lose their glitter.
You're no glutton, or so
you think,
You take wing never
fitter
And return each morning
after.

Wings of Fire. A Piece of Material.

Wings of Fire

The announcement of the coming
Was as wings of St. Elmo's fire,
Blazing haughtily as peacocks
Bursting with infinite desire.

To claim all earthly wealth
Beneath water and scorching soil.
Crushing the opponent
Watching centuries boil,
On Wings of Fire.

History is only a passing of time;
No in-between, no bitter rhyme.
Observed repeat's but stolen design
Claimed by multitudes sought after decline,
On Wings of Fire.

As birds of a feather cling together,
The line of defense never broken
Blocking the intrusive invading eye
All flock to the air not knowing whither,
on Wings of Fire.

Some see their tomorrow
As patterns in the sea,
But cannot dive in
To rescue a friend or flee
From the enemy they should defend,
On Wings of Fire.

They fly with a mourning cry,
And watch their futures die
As night descends its shadows black.
The pickings are slim till dawn is back,
on Wings of Fire.

World Satellite Surveillance

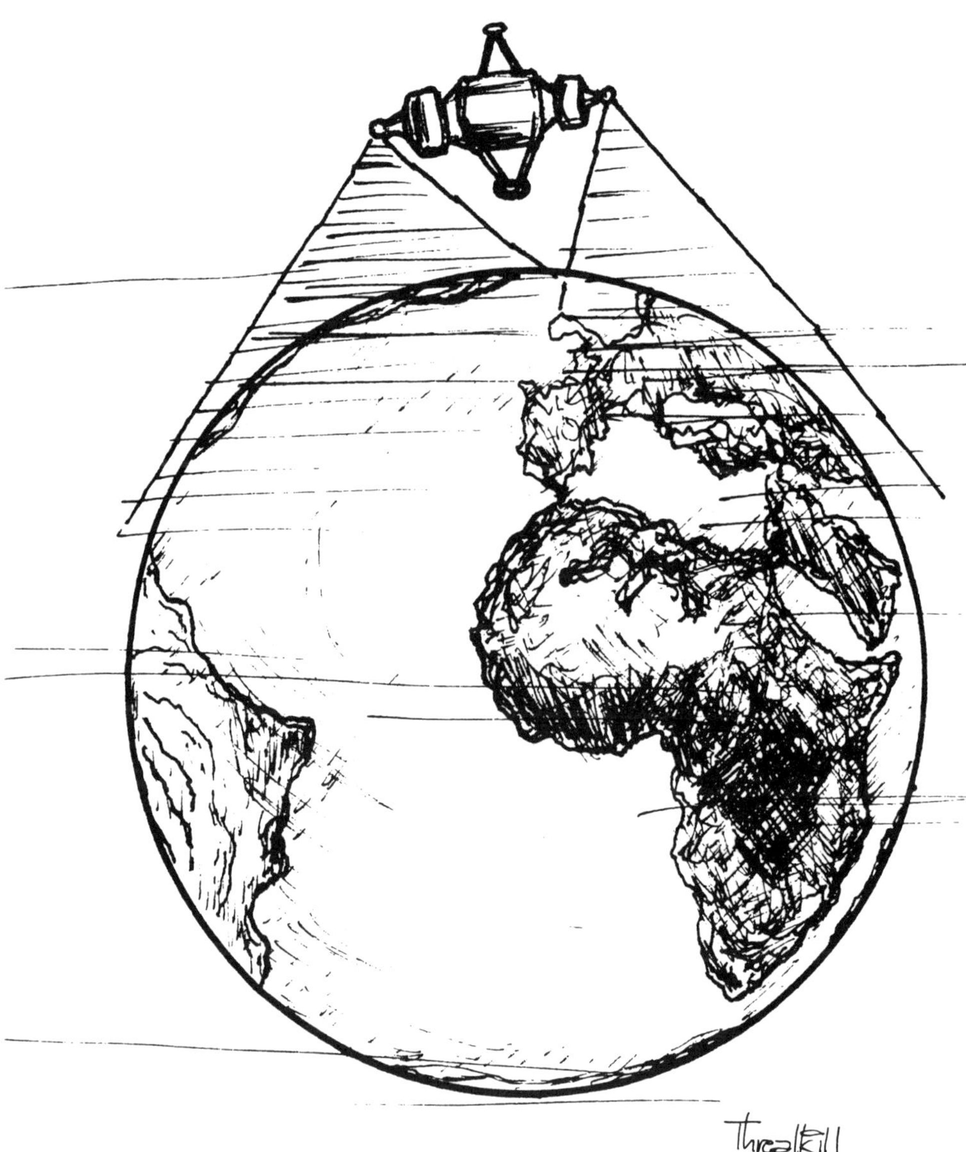

Shades and Shadows of War

Our patriotism is being
tested;
But action is not addressed,
Not even in Congress
With a mindset of
greediness.

The walls of Communism
have come down.
We are scattered in mind
and background
Of where to go, whom
to turn around.

Should one man dictate
the future
Without support
of the people,
Who speak through Congress
Yet endure
A recess, without
projectables?

Threalkill

Who Will Trade?

Who will trade?

Human flesh and oil!

Same as gold and sugar cane;

Commodities to boost the economy.

A constant search for immortality,

Restlessness unbridled,

On the march to fame.

Desert Shield

They've done it again.
They've come to get our women and men
To walk and kill in desert sand,
Deployed with heavy gear
And a blistering demand:
Destroy everything in sight.
If lucky you might
Return and claim a tattered flag
Burned and trampled.
Watch others brag:
This is our all, our native land.
Who needs oil in exchange for
blood?
Who'd take the hand of a brother
Or say to another
You are my friend.
Let us begin again.
Let's try another tactic at
the table.
Let's shake hands as long as we're able
And share the wealth with others.

Children of Palestine

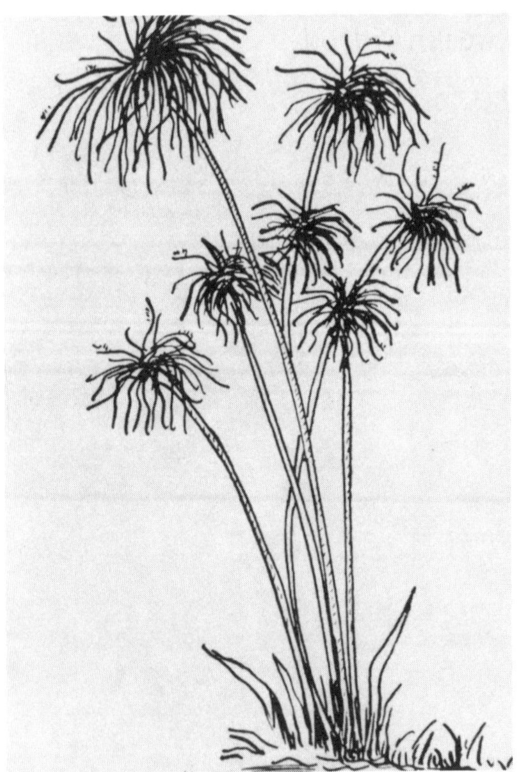

The papyrus from which principal writing material of ancient times was made.

Flowers of Tomorrow

The leaves of yellow,

Red, and brown

Spiraled down

The raindrops.

Wind blown.

Eclipsed.

Their tumbling sails

First on the gale

Landing on soft ground

To be disturbed

and found

Only by time.

Night Watch

The tanks are gathering.

Bunkered in the sand.

Nervous fingers await

command:

The endless call of duty.

See! the moon rises.

Now, we destroy the enemy.

Grief and Mourning

Grief and mourning

Are not the same when faced.

One needs immediate nurturing,

The other time and space.

Both need acknowledging

The facts within our belief.

Both need processing

To work through deepening grief.

Grief and mourning never end

For a loved one so possessed.

They just become less frequent when

We pass through space

And feelings of emptiness.

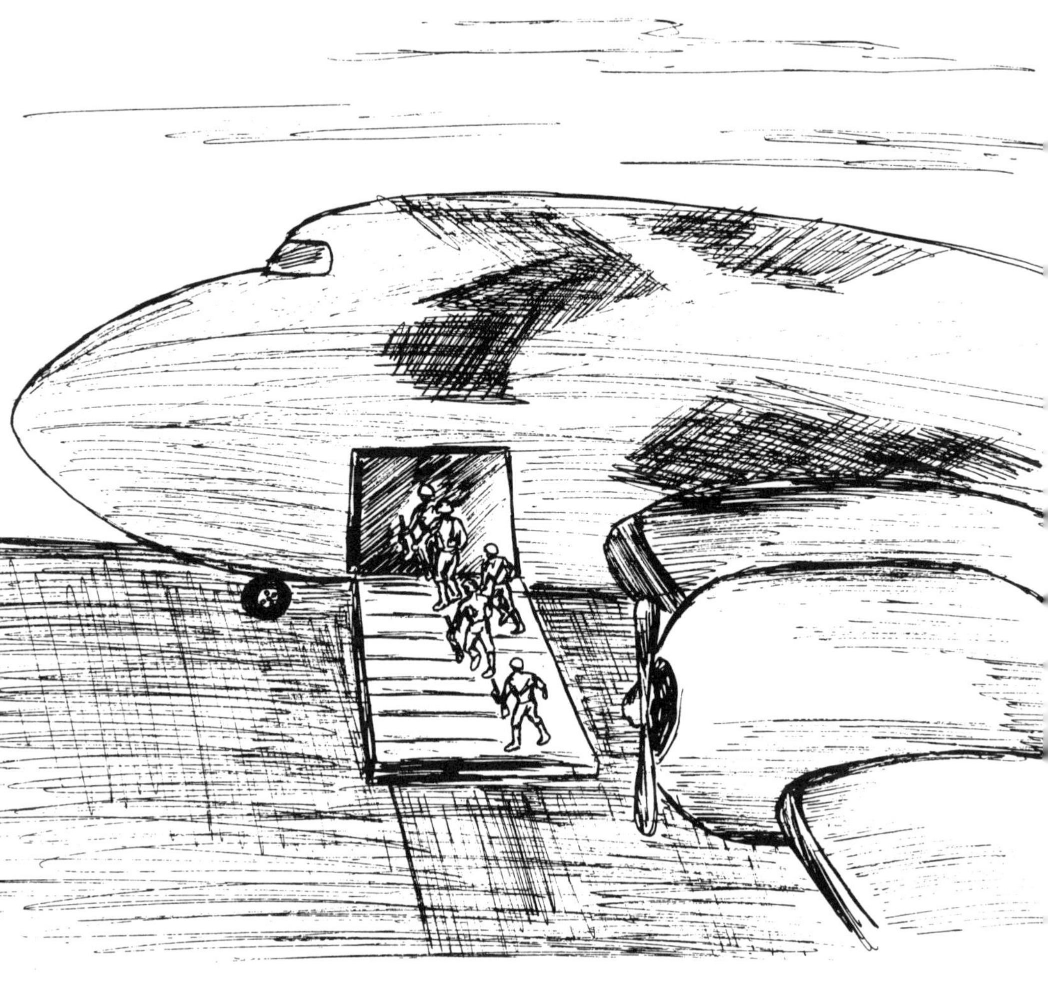

Nature's Constant Rhythm

The swift moving clouds
swept over the fields
Left their shadows on
every leaf yield;
Filled by the under-current
of pungent warm air
That was to become thief
to every sleeping creature's lair.
The rain penetrated the
earth and soon spilled
To rivers that flowed, and unlocked the door
of nature's constant rhythm.

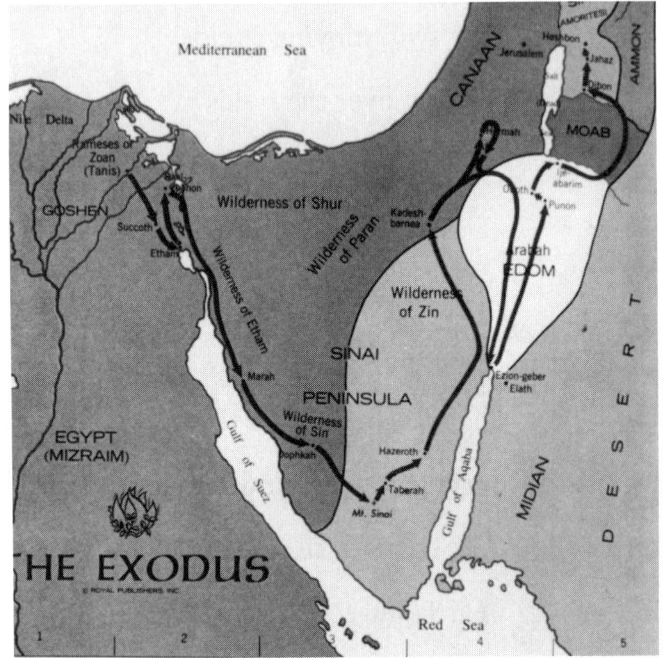

The Exodus

Border Lines of Babylon

Where are Daniel and my Lord?
Once on the Euphrates
Daniel walked with God
and prayed for peach.

Belshazzar is at his
banquet
The shadows are on
the wall.
Who will come to interpret
Before old Babylon falls?

Where are the gardens
Hanging with quiet beauty?
There are no pardons.
There are no prophesies.

Lo, he comes by vision
and God's will
To speak of wicked men
concerning gold, lust, and sin.
"Reveal your dreams grieved
in spirit
Through Him he will
perceive it."

"Babylon is finished
weighed in the balance.
Your bounty falls short.
Diminished.
Heaven is far away,
Seen not even at a glance."

"Your kingdom is in the
shadows.
You are judged, others agree,
Only by God,
Who expects obedience,
Not by me."

"Your kingdom shall fall,
as judgment
You cannot safely
flee,
Turn to God and pay
His price. Repent.
Not for others but
especially for thee."

The commitment was too hard
They could not hear
Tho battles raged at their
feet
Hidden under bridges and
in tunnels very discreet.

Daniel, Oh Daniel, come
forth again;
Pray for all our pardons;
Babylon will fall.
Renew all our gardens."

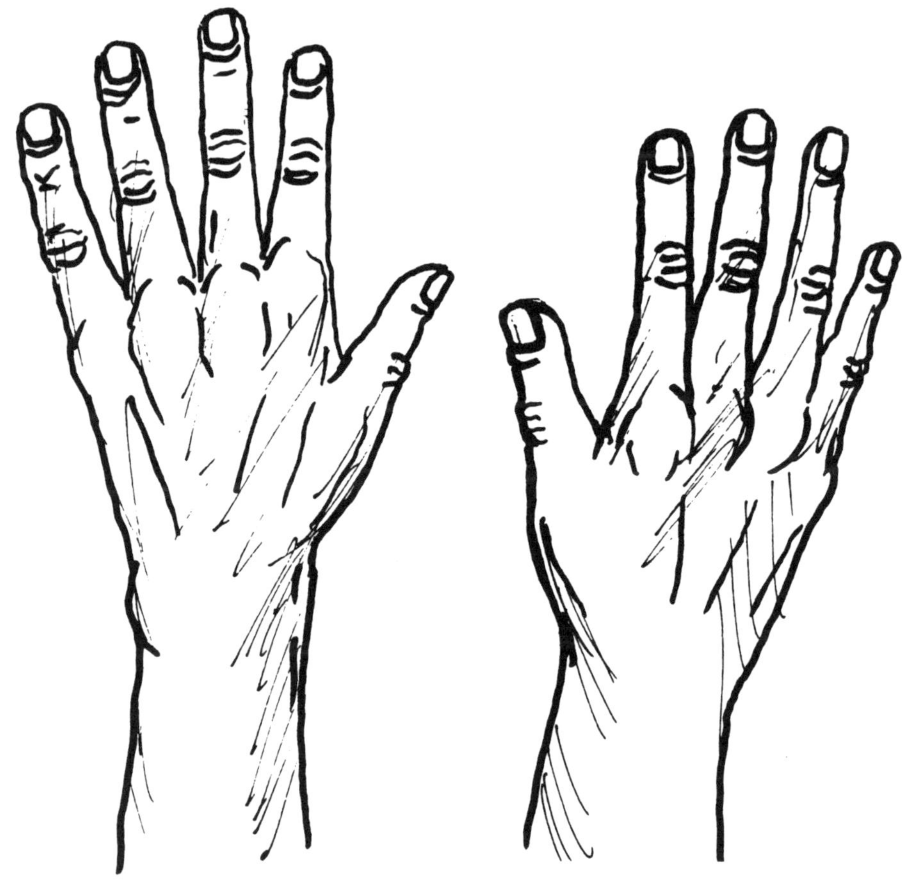

Without Despair

We need to cry
without despair;
To walk alone
with many there;
To find peace within
trust;
To sing in our hearts
As long as we must.

Part II
Early Hours of War

Information Versus Perception

We sit beside our television
sets
To watch a war begin
Not thoroughly rehearsed
but well versed
In technology. Yet,
The enemy does the same
thing.

We watch each other
on a two-way mirror
With communication at its worse
and best
Beyond our limits in
human behavior;
No understanding. We've
regressed.
Information is ahead
of perception
Concerning one being
toward the other;
Our sophistication is
geared toward aggression.
The fight is on for turf, oil,
and power.

The conflicts persist
in moving on
No resolution is in sight.
The age of technology is
Out of reach, and beyond,
Perceived during
Our own marathon.

Possible air strike targets in Iraq

Desert Storm(Head in the Sand)

The element of surprise
and dread
Swept cursedly toward the
rival.
How many children are laying dead?
My heart jumped for
their survival.

The desert sand is cool
at night
A home away, not home.
A place to die
If conquered by
An enemy.
A dungeon hole
to flight.

The stars are bright
with gleaming eyes;
A theatre of moonbeam and
dazzle prolonged.
No guide to a Savior or
holy man or peace,
This has been boldly denied.

As tanks roll by in
dusty storm
Hear the victor raging
with glee
Over the conquered foe.
Left are none.
The threadbare sea
Is drifting toward the
siren wale.
Hear the missiles burst
and roar on
I cannot bear my eyes to see.

Armies of the Coalition

A mighty army of the
coalition
Led by a disciplined
system
Came over the hill to
Crush every ambition.
Every aggressor cut off
to avert Kuwait's doom.

Church of Gethsemane. Site of the Garden.

Church in Bethlehem built over site where Christ was born.

Prayer

Lord, in time of reflection,
Help us unfold all hidden
virtues;
Our wisdom and judgment
ofttimes fail.
Give us patience to
Curb quick action and
torture.
Walk with us by river's
edge,
As we stumble through
the gale.

Time Table

The white amaryllis
kept its appointment
To unfold its bloom
on a winter's night,
Morning came in brief
encounter and went.
But soldiers kept their
fight.

In Israel the sheep lay
sleeping
On hillsides above
the sea.
Close by, the shepherds
were weeping
To see and hear destruction.
People flee.

We cannot stop a force
in motion
Once activated by time
and greed.
Only God on his throne,
hearing every incantation,
Can hurl a mightier
force and succeed.

Oil on Water

Crude Oil in the Persian Gulf

Crude oil in the Persian
Gulf
Irrational as "a dog sitting
on hay,"
Will not deter amphibious
landings on Kuwait's beaches
or bluff
Forces ten miles away.

Why cut off your hand
to spite your mouth
In eco-terrorism, or destroy
systems for decades?
If this is not suicide,
It is fast coming forth.

To divide and conquer neighbors
Is an act or charade.
You cannot gain clout or favor
When an enemy's already made.

Who's Watching the Birds?

The birds are watching
their old habitat
Turn grey and brown where they
once sat.
Trapped in cycles they cannot
flee.
The sky ablaze, their wings
singed hopelessly.
They cannot sing their joys of
home
Or sail in patterned
victory.
They wait to die, let alone
to seek
Their own eternity.

Desert Sand Against the Sea

The desert sand against
the sea
Is spoiled by missiles
and realities
of man's insatiable
greed.
On Candid Camera he
does not smile or think
his Creed

No time for frivolities
in grief and pain.
No long, long breakthrough
of lines
Where the dying and lame
Lie fallen in battle lines
behind.

Can man withstand
an impoverished spirit
In his environs of war
and hate?
We need to focus on
our fate,
As we worship at Armageddon's
gate.

Look at the arrogance of the
Soviet Union,
In its blocking of
Ho Chi Ming,
Nikita Khrushchev,
and the bombing
After the incident of the Gulf of Tankin
Lenid Brezhnev against
imperialism in Asia.
Let's not forget
Mao-Tse-Tung's behavior.
No rhetoric was ever
set.
So here we are, our
laurels down,
Thinking we've accomplished
or conquered all goals.
We are as defenseless as
the open ground
Our heads visible
in desert sand-holes.

Men at Conference Table

Gamesmanship

Our apocalyptic gowns

are aglow,

Caught in our gamesmanship

Of loopholes and potholes.

Politics abound.

Borrowed cash,

Bail-outs

Too complex

For our minds to

amesh.

Our heads are as far

from intransigence

as our idle sex.

Part III

Waiting and Hoping for the Best

Tanks Coming Over the Hill

Gulf Talk

Tuesday here.
Wednesday there.
Long sleepless nights
With rumbles in mid-air.

Dark clouds
Temperature fair.
Jubilant fast talk
Of Iraq's snare.

Flag resistance
Here, There.
Bodies prostrate everywhere
Beyond and over Kuwait's Alliance.

U.S. Brigade
Republic Guard caught
on the road
To the Basra hid-out.

Saddam Hussein
Sad predicament
Thinking long term
Set back by an establishment.

No objective
Good conditions
After the reprieve
Reparations his mission.

All neighbors connected
Even Iran
What will be policy?
Who's in command?

A one-man rule buried
in sand
No legitimacy
Who will take a stand?

Night Vision

We peer to glimpse our
enemy;
Our enemy watches
back.
The same technology
bought from me
Is on the shoulders in
my brother's sack.

He gazes at my artillery
And sizes my strength
to attack.
His vision accommodates
night misery.
His scuds reach their mark,
Aimed at the Bozark.

Bridges Over the Euphrates

Bridges over the Euphrates
are trembling in destruction.
Overhead, missiles target their
key
objective, leaving no
predilection.

Pontoon boats pop up to
answer
The call of frequent annihilability.
Again the monster reveals
his posture
To draw in its dire
propensity.

Tower of the Virgin Mary

Universal Pain

We care about your pain
and sorrow.
Pain is universal.
When loved ones are snatched
from a mother's breast
Our hearts leap too,
in sadness.

When grief and sorrow
pain you,
And you find there is
no relief,
Walk by our side in
believing,
Take our hand and find
peace.

Part IV
The Fighting Begins

Modern Tactics

Thousands of years of blunders.
Hannibal has come back
With modern tactics
To overcome Iraq.

The world is only a speck of sand
Viewed with cosmic-ray eyes,
Every move suspect to the enemies guise
To deploy and wait the unexpected stand.

The indifference of an idle mind,
When threatened, will trimble with fear.
The systolic and diastolic pulse will find
It hard to sink again when night is near.

Release your barren rocks of armour,
Useless against the foe.
Claim only that which is yours, with a firmer
Grip, your fruit of conscious woe.

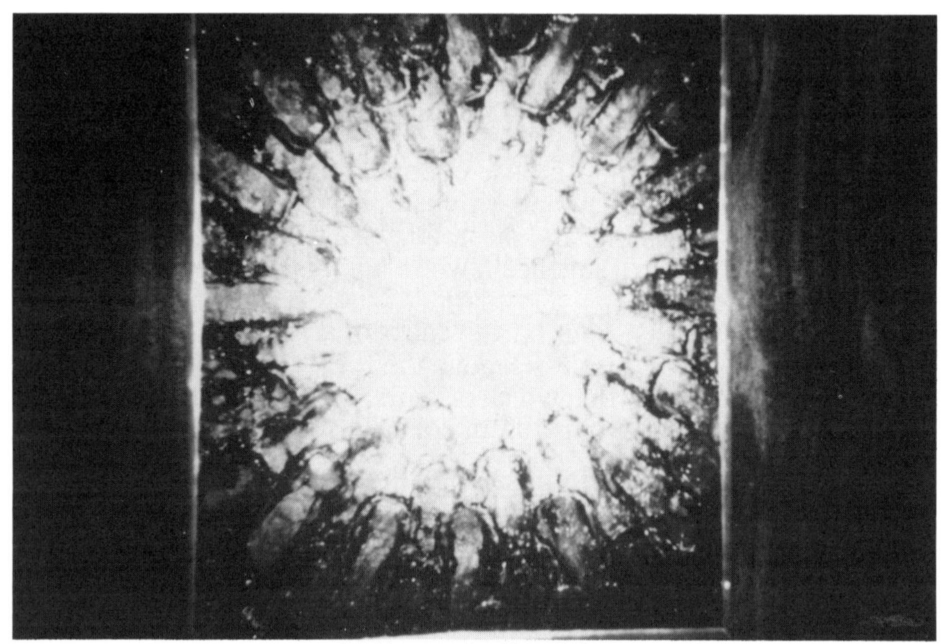

Eclipse of a Particle

Firecrackers: The Fourth of July

Like firecrackers on the Fourth of July
The cruise missiles came
To blaze a dark sky,
And targeted their aim the same.

The people scrambled for cover from heat.
Fire danced a rhythm of last night's repeat.
Hidden on the last floor a reporter or two
Zipped their suits for protection and next que.

CNN's trying to record it all
With mask and covers against the wall.
Citizens are watching and calling the shots,
Trying to referee a television plot.

Are you watching Dear God of all?
Please send your angels inside these walls.
Your children are trapped in Satan's snare;
There is suffering and death everywhere.

Women at the Wall

Our Prayer

Our prayers rang out strong and clear
To alleviate every emotion, every fear
Of loosing our loved ones,
and total encountering
Of all our hopes and dreams begun.

There is no other force greater
Than a hopeless people
calling louder and louder
For release of pain and sorrow,
For peace, grace, mercy,
and a watchful eye
for tomorrow.

May history of this scorched land
Be consecrated again with new ideas and new revelations
To spread the word of God's steadfast love again
Rather than hate, greed, and possession.

Wings of Fire. A Piece of Material.

Iron Rain

The rockets rained down
On the blistering frontier
As ground fighting drew near.
Tears rolled down with
mourning and fear.

The soldier said, “don’t cry, my son,
Our God is very near,
His children are not smitten."
Long written
Made absolutely clear.

Prepare to cross the border
They’re coming slow but sure.
Flee if you must disappear
To the North Pole or farther.

Protect your head
When rockets come near.
A nightmare scenario
Is in progress. Almost here.

Threlkill

Earth Scorching

The oil wells are burning.
They scorch the surface earth.
No living thing moving.
No chance for rebirth.

If we canst have it,
It surely is not yours.
Drop all mandates
No condition goes.

Mid-day is waiting
Space and time,
A limited ultimatum
Your move next has begun.

Run to the border
Sling open the gate.
Schamal the sandunes
Hail your fate.

Dome of the Rock

Songs of Despair

Behold! The birds

And animals of the sea.

Their eyes are pleading,

Rescue me!

From overflow and spill of oil,

Have you heard songs

of despair?

Seen their toil

Coming forth strong to offend

You,

To prick all conscious

everywhere?

Shave in a Wash Pan

Shave in a wash pan.
Remnant of the past.
Poised behind banks
of sand
Hidden from Saudi eyes
Reflected in glass.

So precious are the
jewels of water
Once free to flow and
cleanse the soul
Now dried up or
rationed as we barter
Our shaven heads
to again control.

Nomads

Sandunes of Death

Sandunes of death
No place to hide.
Castles overhead.
Life denied.

Fire Chariots are looming
To take you from your veil
Stand by the gates of perpetual hell
Twist your hands and pray for
a miracle.

No wailing wall.
People will not come.
Kneel for yourself.
Await allah home.

De-robe your abhors and
Chadors
Blowing in the wind.
Your only defense,
Cannot shield Saddam Hussein.

Livestock Near the Sea of Galilee

Parting the Waters

Look out at the sea!
It's running with blood
Not from a miracle.
It's my real tears a-flood.

Look out at the ocean!
This time it's real.
The oil-slick is drifting
Toward my neighbor's field.

Look out at the skylift!
The drama begins
It starts with the children.
When will it end?

Where are the friends?
Who's in attend?
On whom shall we depend?
Who has a hand to lend?

Look out at the mountains!
They crumble in dimensional
motion.
Run for the forest!
It's reflected in the ocean.

Diplomatic Flurry or Ultimatum

Time and awaiting its effect,
Can shake all foundations
so set.
Time to contemplate Iraq's
move
Time for embassy's to rush
to prove
A mediator or third party
contact,
To bring the solution to
fruition not look back.
Remarks unwarranted,
this date
Cannot communicate,
Instructions await.
Interpretations in detail
Too long to digest; to no
avail
To convince or make
a compromise;
Effect a peaceful
withdrawal in disguise.
Time and choices lost
to initiate.
Possibilities exhausted
can't wait.
Cannot fully and openly
explain,
Burning of oil fields
so disdained.
Green light, red light,
all doors closed.
No turning point or flight.
Now begins the fight.

Part V
The Fighting Ends

Oil on Water

Predictions

The patterns of oil
On moving waters
Did not reveal
Their many secrets
Of unpredictable
Things now slaughtered.

Birds could not fly
in patterns
nor wet
Their wings if matted
with oil;
and yet,
On a clear night
The stars burnt forth
To predict the movement
of gods and earth.

It Is Finished!
(After Six Weeks)

It is finished!
You cannot flee.
A coup-de-grace.
You did not welcome
the plea.

Weary docile men
From infernos of sand
Crept from their prisons
And bowed on command.

Women at the wall
waiting patiently.
A sad dilemma.
Both sides feel the fall.
Diplomacy and Solidarity
Come to the front.
Objectives mount
And bring peace to account.

A four day war
Liberation without flaw.
My brother is bleeding,
My country heeding.

The joys of freedom
unbridled and late.
The flag will raise
Its colors of praise.

Men Surrendering

Quiet Surrender

I saw them kiss their
enemy's hand,
Raising hands above
Their head bands
Praising the enemy,
not their god
For capture, and perhaps
a new start.

No more eating of grass
and weeds,
No absence of water except
rain reeds
Bitter with excreta.
A sign of nature
Soaked up swiftly,
Snatched willfully.

They came by the thousands
over the hill
Begging for mercy,
Longings fulfilled,
By the thousands
They came to weep.
Surrendered quietly
and worshiped at his feet.

Swish Goes the Storm

Swish goes the wind
over desert sand.
Cool is the bitter night
In a foxhole fight.

Warm is the morning
But no place to hide.
Swish goes the wind
All comfort denied.

Swish go the missiles
To destroy the foe,
Landing their mark
Close to my door.

Swish go the people
Frightened and unfed.
Open are the sandunes,
Buddies lying dead.

Fifty pounds of heavy gear,
Hundred twenty in racksack.
The mind and body cringe in fear
Time too short to look back.

Swish, go wheels to enter the gate,
Swish, the fireballs to enter Kuwait,
Swish, the war heads, the battle's begun.
The battle is won.
Quiet are the people.

Come home, my daughters.
Come home, my sons.

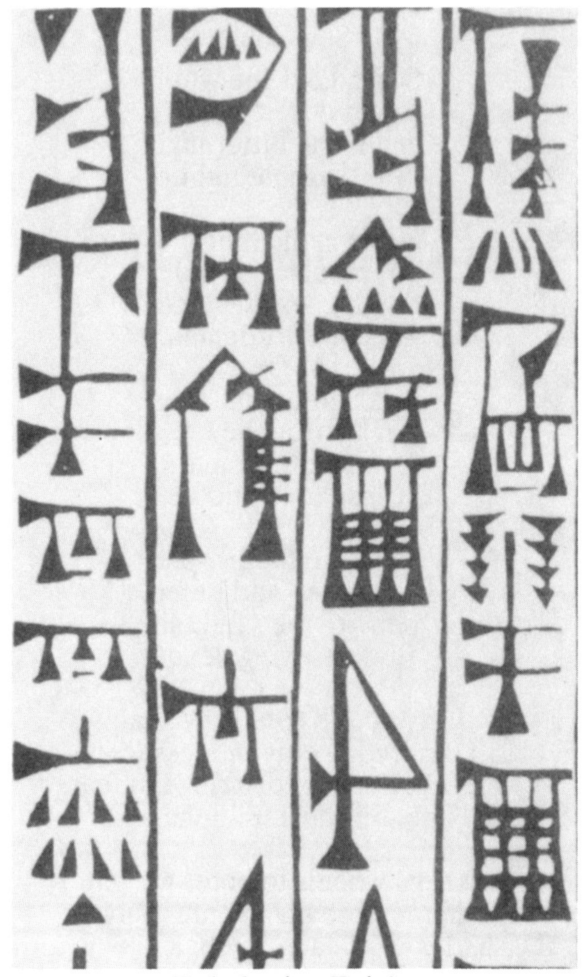
Babylonian Brick

Pictures on the Wall

I once looked at those
pictures on the wall
At Babylon, and wondered what
they told their gods when people
Bowed in prayer throughout
the day
Long before empires declined,
What did they say?

Save me?
Cover me?
Deliver me?
Whither shall I flee?

Some nations should be
proud they stayed
To communicate their evidence,
of having been in the parade.

How could they abandon their
gardens of romance,
Dream-walk in the open
sand,
Leave their children on
demand,
Or make new idle kingdoms?

Where else do visions come
true,
lions lay down with
lambs,
Or hands of prophets build
ships
To sail the flood at
Noah's grip?

Where else do shepherd
boys sing
To lyrics, softly larking
Tone on tone, building
patterns of music
With chords and words of Arabic?

These were future nations –
Lights that pass before
tomorrow
With dreams of hope, but
Begging sorrow.

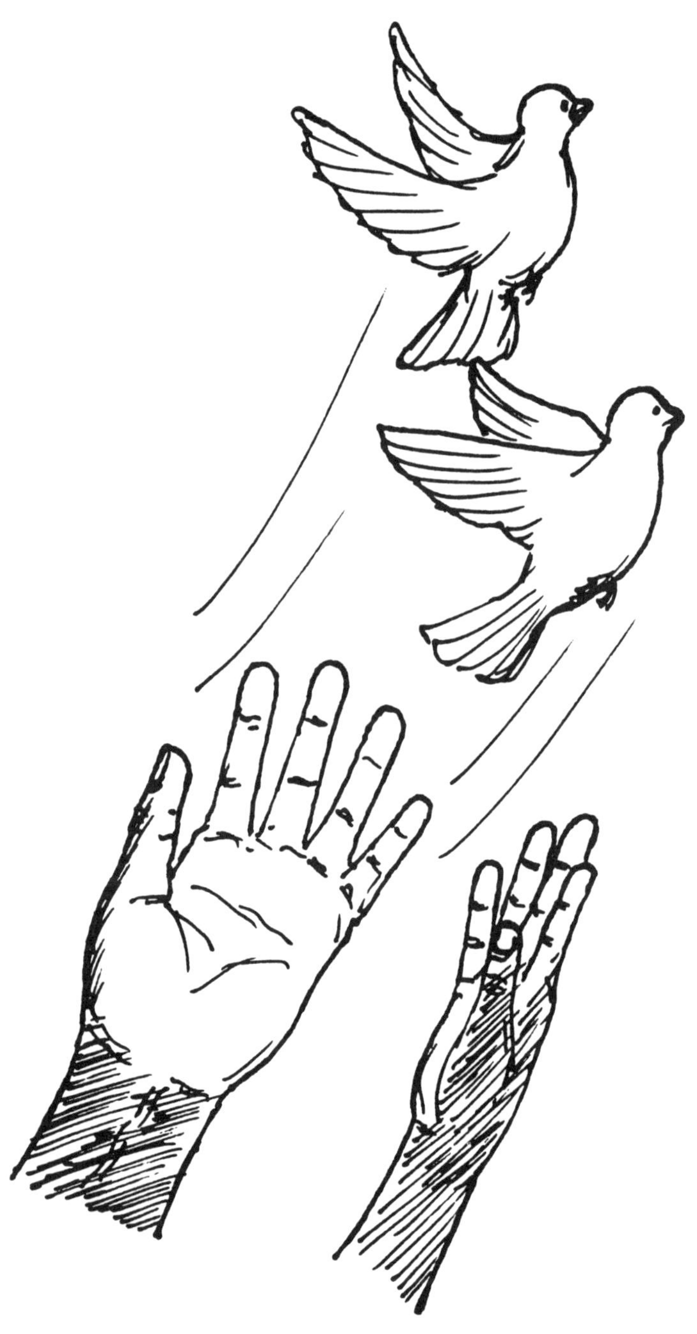

White Dove

A semblance of peace
Has been released,
Not an Olive leaf
But hopeful expression increased.

A white dove
Between the palm
Seeks direction of love
How shall it come? What form?

Exuberance of hope
Beams on each face.
What depth and scope
What subliminal grace.

Democracy waits
Each man his own,
A living dream to contemplate
Summoned longings never too soon.

Fly little angel
Sing your missioned flight.
Dip each wing as you
climb the gales
On winds of joy to prove
each right.

Wing of Dove

The people gathered 'round to see
One man with dove in hand to flee
To ocean's edge where freedom dwells
And return the message that all is well.

Peace is somewhere on the wind
That love and hope will return to end
Great destruction, and men who fight
And die for naught; not knowing right.

God grant that the angel's wing of dove
Will dip its quill on the edge of love
Write each commandment high above
To be read in the hearts of men who love.

Part VI
After the Storm

Liberation from the Storm

Many men needed to prove

their worth;

A raison d'etre upon

this earth

A liberation from

the self

And all wonders of

life and death.

There is no competition

greater

Than a man seeking

love which slowly begins

Outside of self,

A fighter

Punching at the wind

When there is no one to

defend.

New Direction of Time

A new direction of time
has come
To mend the bridges we
made; and from
That time, we cross to meet
And wash all ills beneath
our feet.

A new direction of time
has come
To assert itself and
conquer some
Old wounds that fester
when left unclean,
and slow the process
to heal unforeseen.

A new direction of time
has come
To leave behind the
shadowed face of gloom
to seek new wonders
of understanding and grace
Our future with welcomed
peace.

Forgiveness

Then Peter came up and said to Him, "Lord, how often shall my brother sin against me, and I forgive him? As many as seven times?" Jesus said to him, "I do not say to you seven times, but seventy times seven"

(Matthew 18:21-22, Revised Standard Version of the Bible).

Prayer

Lord, we may not
see your land again
Except when televised
by anxious men.
Then, eyes will attest
To the potential beauty
Of gardens hanging
In their habitat of bounty.

Threlkill

Kuwait

The sun cannot
Bless this land.
It does not wait
Tho colors grand
For a rainbow
Through the clouds.
Oil on this land
Betrays its use and demands,
Even swirled in air.
A rainbow cannot prepare
For a bright tomorrow.

Destruction

A Harvest Of Splinters

We encouraged a fight,

A political coup.

The time was right

To stay our power

And see it through.

To settle all doubt

Of commanding clout.

A fixed power

At the last hour

Of a wounded economy

Steeped in fantasy.

A nuclear winter

In summer heat

A harvest of splinters –

We gather our feat.

Part VII
Continued Global Unrest And Destruction

Wings of Fire. A Piece of Material.

War!

War!

War!

War!

What are we fighting for?

More!

More!

More!

Global destruction to dust.

Fear!

Passion!

Lust!

Flowers in the Snow

Winter is running
Far behind time;
First the snowflakes
Then the sun shines.
Who knows when
To fling the covers
Put on more
Before starting over?
Trees budding
As flowers before,
Frozen after
A light snow,
Buried beneath
Their bursting door,
Drooping their heads
To lift no more.
Their pungent beds
Fused in the wind,
No more tomorrows
To watch seasons begin,
All moved back
Too late for summer,
They all look alike
But must sleep their own winter.

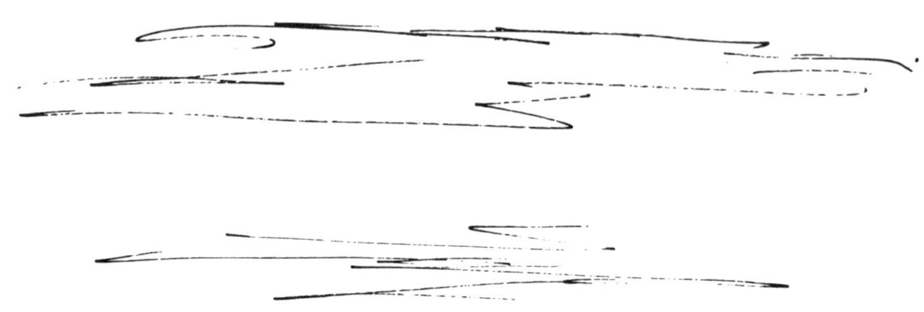

Broken Cross

Forgive me

If I have wounded

Your conscious,

Your self image,

Your spirituality;

Embarrassed your cross

Seemingly broken

In understanding.

I cannot render

Thou withered away

Your crucified faith,

But I will beseech

And rejoice your forgiveness

In your creation of love;

Love's everlasting wonderment,

But most of all, your smile.

In Retrospect

In retrospect we come to know
The seasons as they come and go.
People pass by and wars overcome
Then break the mold of greed for some.

Come let us sing of jubilance and hope;
Tie a yellow ribbon; survey the scope;
Take the future as it is;
Live our lives not as others see us.
We've reached a pinnacle and
heard tell
When neighbors believe in neighbors,
Trusting, they leave no scars.
And in the name of freedom, all is well.

Cedars of Lebanon

Desert Calm

I will steal away and feel the quiet
That stillness which come from inner peace.
From all the pouring out, I will find release
From pain felt after destruction, defied.

I will sleep again tho the weariness lies deep
Inside my pillows of sorrow and turbulence
This will be rippled away in recompense
Through silence, and with it my soul
He keeps.

Threlkill

Grudges

Ashes are still smoldering
Palestinians and Israelis are still holding
Their grudges. Whose space belongs to whom?
Whom are they taking from?

How can they push each other
Far enough in anger
Brother against brother
Guarding a strip of land called
Mother?

Worn and torn through the ages
Killing each other and turning pages
Of time they cannot spare
And problems no other nation wishes
to share?

Tumbleweed

We are as tumbleweed drifting across sand;
Only the wind knows where we will land.
In its message of whispered refrain,
We will drift beyond all flowers and rain.

Some buried beneath towers and steeples
With greed as their master of all the people,
Lost in time and silently weeping.
Others drifting with the wind, never seeking.

Tolerance and Compassion

Tolerance and compassion?
We fought tooth and nail to gain them both
And reaped instead
Individual expression and greed.
We feed on the demise of others
And hope for the rebirth
Of group ideas to triumph over
Political issues while we plant the seed
To free our spines of morbid passion
to succeed.

Victory

It is said that victory is sweet.
If true, why do I feel so incomplete,
So unfulfilled, empty, and sad,
Weary of war, and of those who destroy
half mad?

It seems we are prisoners of self
When we prey on others or devour what's left,
Tho we bury our spoils in the burning sand,
We see the after birth of monster or man.

We breed the remembrance of waste and time
As we thunder ourselves on evening prime time.
Our hearts are purple around our necks;
Badges of honor not proved in effect.

A distance away grows dim to sight
When we forget our loss, yet our right.
Rain keeps falling on the just, we fight,
But the scars remain as horrors that ignite.

People and War

People and war are like the rain.

They return with the seasons over and over again

With no thought of destruction or pain

Just a fact of life accepted. No gain.

Wars die down

Rise up and return with a bound,

Camouflaged and decalletaged

Honored for fame and dodged.

They are politicized and dramatized

On stages as the curtain rises.

Masked for gas, or disguised, then fought again

People worship them, but their friend

they feign.

Ode to War

We cut down a tree
An emotional defeat
To satisfy a need
We often repeat.

We destroy one another
And take our lead
From a hunger unsolved
An innocence we feed.

A Changin'

Rappers rap
While countries die.
Children cry and
Not know why.

Beepers beep
And often deny
A Changin' as they sleep.
Others walk by.

Waters creep
Above the edges.
December leeps
Bringing data and pledges

Economic dreams,
Never what's seen.
Babies' lives lost by means
Of neglect. No one confessing.

The ocean heaves
While jobs sink,
But waters recede
At planets brink.

Hunger spreads
As blowing wind.
A prayer is said;
We seek a friend.

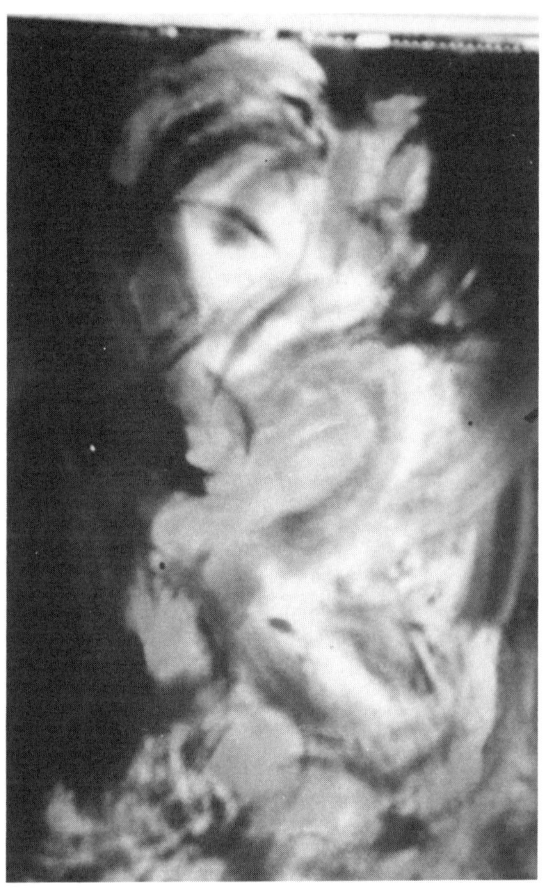

Fire Dance

Sword Dancers

Watch the sword dancers perform their rite
As they cap the fires on the last oil blight
Swirled above the awesome clouds
A black ribbon risen beyond the crowd.

It will perform no more,
Snuffed out by a lancing blow.
We celebrate in our flowing gowns
As we step forward, our future crowned.

The People of Russia

The people of Russia couldn't afford to change
And so they rebelled against the new
And staged a coup,
Although repelled.
They faced the resistance
Of Yeltsin and Crew:
Time and the economy
Were too slow
For pent up emotions
And slavery of men.
A taste of freedom
Whet tongues for more
Held out by Gorbachev
On a platter of show.
Conspirators thought their
"Scuds" were real
Aimed at the opposition of time.
Time never stands still
As the people revealed
And so goes history as often revealed;
Power is given to demand and will
While independence begs for legitimate control,
But they want the blessing of a strong hand
To guide and decide the best order for the whole.
So, where to next Mr. Gorbechev and Yeltsin?
The Baltic states are requesting
Do not wait!
A taste for freedom, you must abate.

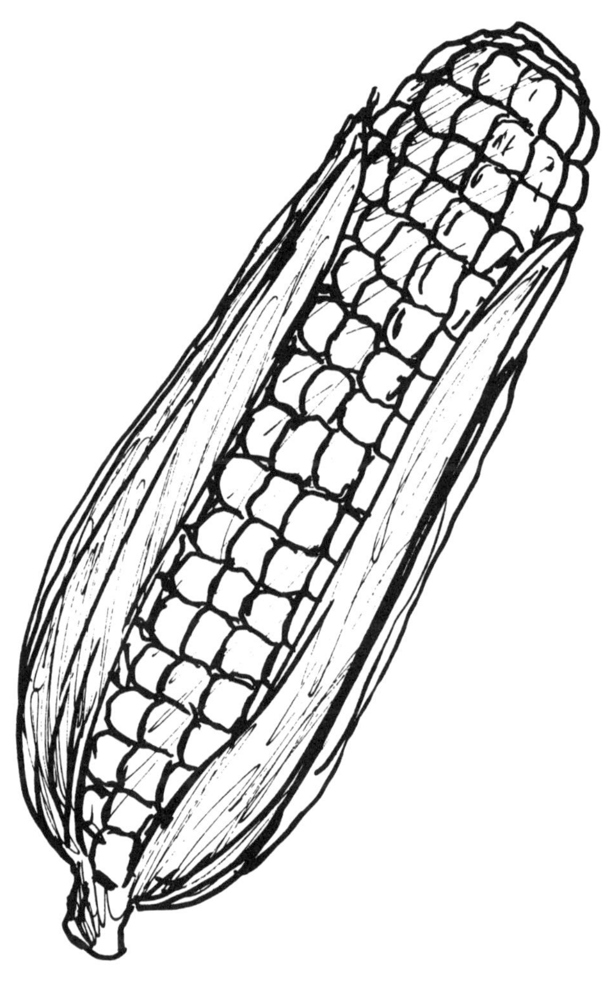

Feeding the Multitudes

Will we feed our brother
From food trampled in dust?
Or will we take from one another
And feed the multitude of trust?

Who will eat the spoils of war
Left over from the Persian Gulf?
Russia is on the road to starvation's door
And we gloat our conquest as proof.

Will the mold from grain be enough
To save the starving nations?
Or will we grab from pigs their hooves
And scream that we've bribed salvation?

Faith

Faith heals the troubled heart.

There is always a tomorrow.

Belief comes when there's healing after

sorrow

And washes away the tears of the heart.

He who never believes

Is always left waning;

His heart and eyes are paining;

Truth faining and there is no relief.

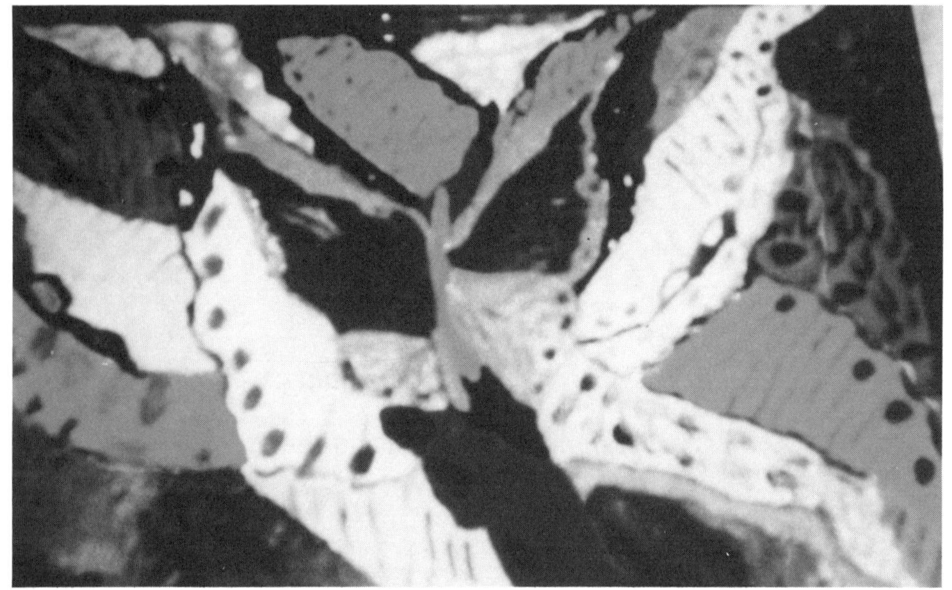

Freedom

Is There Ever Victory After War?

Is there ever victory after war?

Only time will tell:

When the human heart has healed;

When love has been revealed;

When greed has vanished beyond earthly things;

And birds are free to sing.

About the Author

Mattie Shavers Johnson is an accomplished educator, lecturer, author, poet, and musician. She has taught at the elementary through college levels, written, and performed both piano compositions and poetry in a variety of settings and on many occasions.

She has produced a community guide book and published several chap books. Her early public speaking earned honors in high school and college.

Johnson is a native of Garland Community, DeKalb, Texas, the eighth child (a twin) of four brothers and six sisters born to Robert S. Shavers and Laura Garland Shavers.

She earned a Bachelor of Science degree from Tennessee State University at Nashville, Tennessee, Master of Science from Hunter College at New York City, and Master of Science in Public Health from Meharry Medical College at Nashville. As a concerned educator, Johnson established a scholarship in the name of her parents at Fisk University also at Nashville. Her alma mater, Meharry Medical College honored Johnson with a scholarship in her name for her many contributions to the institution. She has also given valuable service as a Girl Scout board member and a choir director of music. Johnson is a member of St. Andrews Presbyterian Church.

After thirty successful years in the teaching profession, she devotes her time exclusively to her writing and volunteer work.

Johnson is married to Charles W. Johnson, M.D., Vice President Emeritus of Meharry Medical College. The Johnsons live in Nashville. They are the parents of Charles W., Jr., Phillip N., and Livette Suzanne.